WHERE PEOPLE LIVE

LIFE ON THE COAST

WRITTEN BY
Noah Leatherland

KidHaven PUBLISHING

Published in 2025 by
KidHaven Publishing, an Imprint of
Greenhaven Publishing, LLC
2544 Clinton St., Buffalo, NY 14224

Written by: Noah Leatherland
Edited by: Rebecca Phillips-Bartlett
Designed by: Ker Ker Lee

Cataloging-in-Publication Data

Names: Leatherland, Noah, 1999-.
Title: Life on the coast / Noah Leatherland.
Description: Buffalo, NY : KidHaven Publishing, 2025. | Series: Where people live | Includes glossary and index.
Identifiers: ISBN 9781534549227 (pbk.) | ISBN 9781534549234 (library bound) | ISBN 9781534549241 (ebook)
Subjects: LCSH: Coasts--Juvenile literature. | Seashore ecology--Juvenile literature. | Seashore--Recreational use--Juvenile literature. | Seaside architecture Juvenile literature
Classification: LCC GB453.L38 2025 | DDC 307.0914'6--dc23

Manufactured in the United States of America

CPSIA compliance information: Batch #CW25KH
For further information contact Greenhaven Publishing LLC at 1-844-317-7404.

Please visit our website, www.greenhavenpublishing.com.
For a free color catalog of all our high-quality books, call toll free 1-844-317-7404 or fax 1-844-317-7405.

Find us on

IMAGE CREDITS

All images are courtesy of Shutterstock.com. With thanks to Getty Images, Thinkstock Photo and iStockphoto.
Cover – tandaV, Marty Jean-Louis, HappyPictures. Alien Character – HappyPictures. Background throughout – Picksell. 4–5 – 19 STUDIO, Jacob Boomsma, leoks, Nuria Kreuser. 6–7 – vololibero, ThomBal, Patricia Elaine Thomas. 8–9 – StacieStauffSmith Photos, VIAVAL TOURS. 10–11 – DnDavis, Yingna Cai, oneinchpunch, EQRoy, Felix Mizioznikov, travelview, travelview. 12–13 – Fominayaphoto, Terry Kelly. 14–15 – Kwangmoozaa, Andrey Sayfutdinov. 16–17 – Wangkun Jia, Monkey Business Images. 18–19 – Viktoriia Hnatiuk Daniel Hoz. 20–21 – Druid007, ggw. 22–23 – Wangkun Ji, rangizzz, 19 STUDIO, HappyPictures.

CONTENTS

WORDS THAT LOOK LIKE **THIS** CAN BE FOUND IN THE GLOSSARY ON PAGE 24.

WELCOME TO EARTH

Humans have made homes on almost every part of Earth. Their **SETTLEMENTS** can be found in cold places, hot places, wet places, and dry places. In this episode, we will be looking at coasts.

WHAT HUMANS MEAN

SETTLEMENT: Anywhere that a group of people builds a place to live

WHAT ON EARTH IS A COAST?

A coast is an area of land that is beside the ocean. Not every part of the coast is the same. Some parts might have sandy beaches. Others might have tall, rocky cliffs.

Different kinds of settlements can be found along the coast. Many humans have made their homes there. There are villages, towns, and even entire cities that have been built by the coast.

SAN DIEGO, CALIFORNIA

WHERE ARE THEY GOING?

Many of the people found at the coast live there. Some coastal settlements also get lots of **TOURISTS**. They might have come a long way to visit the coast.

WHAT HUMANS MEAN

TOURISTS: People who visit another place for fun

With many people living along the coast and even more coming to visit, coastal settlements need lots of **FACILITIES**. All of those humans need to eat, sleep, exercise, play, and learn, after all!

WHAT HUMANS MEAN

FACILITIES: Places, buildings, and equipment needed for certain activities

WHAT IS ON THE COAST?

Following humans around the coast led me to some very interesting places. Here are some of the places I went.

STORES AND OTHER BUSINESSES

PIERS

PLACES OF WORSHIP

Humans who belong to a **religion** use these places to **pray** and **worship**.

BOARDWALKS

HOUSES

PORTS

SCHOOLS

Ports are where ships bringing **goods** from other places arrive.

HAVING FUN ON THE COAST

Humans love to have fun. Coastal settlements have facilities for the **RESIDENTS** and tourists to enjoy themselves. As well as being fun, these facilities also help humans stay fit and healthy.

WHAT HUMANS MEAN

RESIDENTS: People who live in an area

Being beside the sea gives coastal settlements lots of natural spaces for humans to enjoy. This brings many tourists to the coast. They can have fun on land or on the water.

Humans stand on boards to ride waves. Amazing!

SHOPPING ON THE COAST

Stores are an important part of human settlements. Humans can get everything they need to live from stores. They can also get extra things to treat themselves!

Shores on the coast might be different from shops in other places. Some stores sell things to tourists, such as **souvenirs**. Some sell things that can be used in the coast's natural spaces.

TOWN HALLS

Just like other settlements, coastal **COMMUNITIES** often come together and have meetings to decide on how things are run. A coastal community might have a town hall or somewhere similar to meet.

A TOWN HALL

WHAT HUMANS MEAN

COMMUNITIES: Groups of people who have something in common, such as where they live

Town hall meetings give residents a chance to talk about what is happening in their community. Residents get to talk to **local** leaders who make big decisions in the settlement.

SCHOOLS

These children are climbing onto a big yellow bus. I wonder how many of them can fit.

The bus is taking them to school. Coastal settlements might have one school or many schools. It depends on how many people live there.

There are different schools for humans of different ages. Some people keep going to school when they are adults to continue learning. More education can help humans get different kinds of jobs.

BUSINESSES ON THE COAST

Businesses are important parts of any settlement. They give jobs to residents and bring in money from other places. Settlements are usually first built around some kind of **INDUSTRY**.

WHAT HUMANS MEAN

INDUSTRY: The people, places, and work involved in making money

For coastal communities, their main businesses might involve the ocean. Many coastal settlements were built around fishing industries. Some have grown around places where ships came to **trade**.

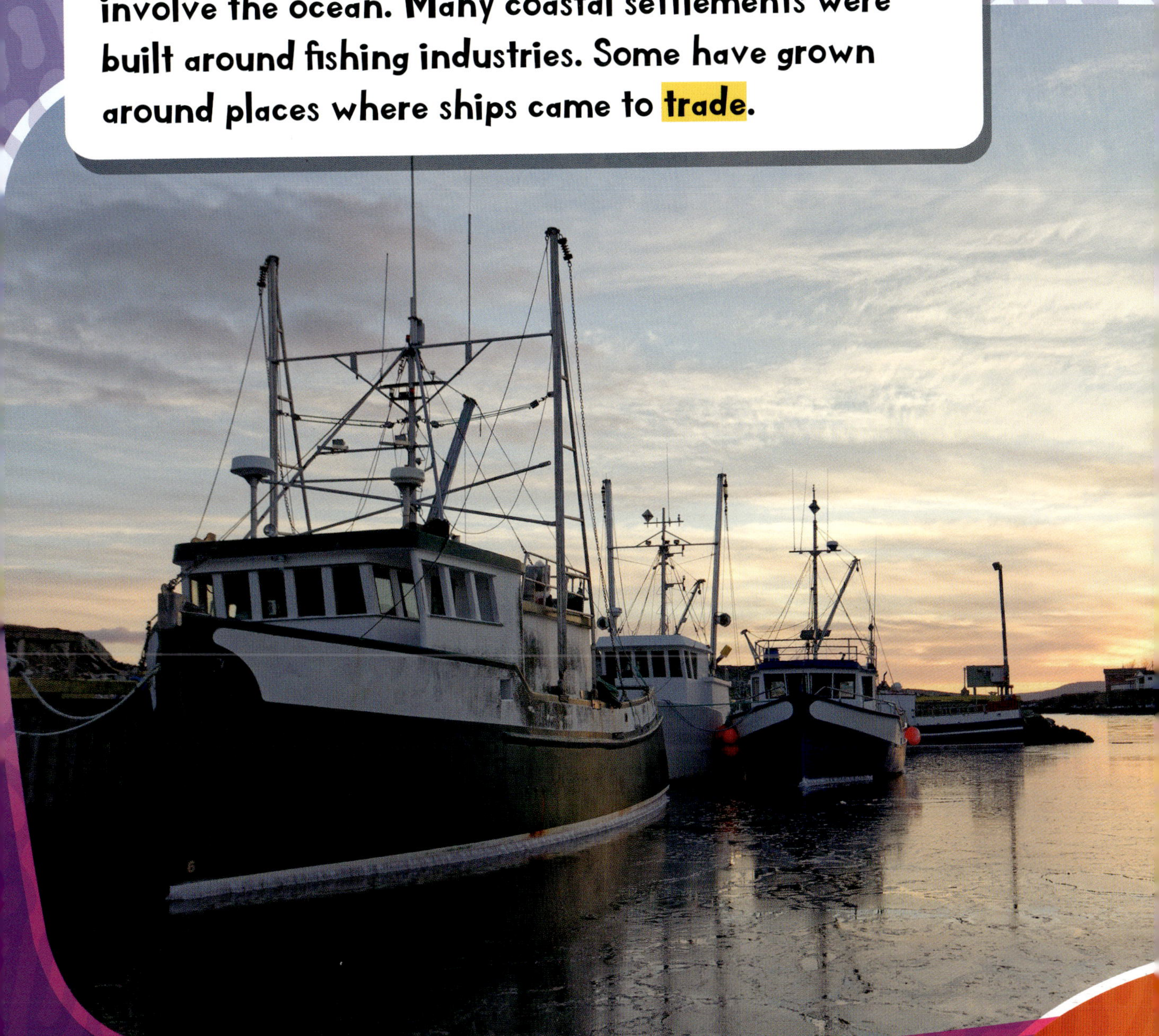

TUNE in NEXT WEEK

Well, viewers, aren't coasts interesting? Lots of people live there, and many more come to visit. There are all kinds of things to do on the land and in the ocean.

Whether you make your home by the coast, in the countryside, or in the middle of a city, they can all be connected by roads, rivers, and railways. The coast could be a nice place to live... if you are a human!

GLOSSARY

GOODS things that are bought and sold

LOCAL relating to the area near where someone lives

NATURAL found in nature and not made by people

PRAY to talk to a god or gods of a chosen belief

RELIGION an organized set of beliefs usually centered around a god or gods

SOUVENIRS objects people keep that remind them of somewhere they visited

TRADE to buy and sell items

WORSHIP a religious act where a person expresses praise for a god or gods

INDEX